CHEETAHS VS. GAZELLES

FOOD CHAIN FIGHTS

SARAH ROGGIO

Lerner Publications ◆ Minneapolis

To my writing group—for 25 years of feedback, friendship, and fun!

Lerner Publications Company
An imprint of Lerner Publishing Group, Inc.
241 First Avenue North
Minneapolis, MN 55401 USA

For reading levels and more information, look up this title at www.lernerbooks.com.

Main body text set in Aptifer Sans LT Pro.
Typeface provided by Linotype AG.

Editor: Angel Kidd **Designer:** Kim Morales

Library of Congress Cataloging-in-Publication Data

Names: Roggio, Sarah, author.
Title: Cheetahs vs. gazelles : food chain fights / Sarah Roggio.
Description: Minneapolis : Lerner Publications, 2025. | Series: Predator vs. prey | Includes bibliographical references and index. | Audience: Ages 8–11 | Audience: Grades 4-6 | Summary: "Cheetahs are the world's fastest land animals. How do gazelles escape these speedy predators? Young learners will uncover the weapons and defenses of each animal and discover who rules the savanna"— Provided by publisher.
Identifiers: LCCN 2024008067 (print) | LCCN 2024008068 (ebook) | ISBN 9798765647295 (lib. bdg.) | ISBN 9798765656914 (epub)
Subjects: LCSH: Cheetah—Juvenile literature. | Thomson's gazelle—Juvenile literature. | Cheetah—Behavior—Juvenile literature. | Thomson's gazelle—Defenses—Juvenile literature. | Predation (Biology)—Juvenile literature.
Classification: LCC QL737.C23 R6645 2025 (print) | LCC QL737.C23 (ebook) | DDC 599.64/69—dc23/eng/20240415

LC record available at https://lccn.loc.gov/2024008067
LC ebook record available at https://lccn.loc.gov/2024008068

ISBN 979-8-7656-6213-7 (pbk.)

Manufactured in the United States of America
1-1010992-53169-5/31/2024

TABLE OF CONTENTS

CHAPTER 1

SCRAMBLE IN THE SERENGETI

THE SUN IS RISING OVER THE SERENGETI. A herd of Thomson's gazelles grazes on the dry grass of the African national park. They flick their black tails back and forth while they eat. Every few seconds, they lift their heads to look around. Gazelles have no place to hide on the flat, open plains. They must keep a close watch for predators.

Nearby, a cheetah watches from a rocky hill. The cheetah studies the herd and spots a small gazelle. This is her target. The cheetah crouches down, then crawls through the grass toward the group.

A herd of Thomson's gazelles grazes on the plains.

A cheetah watches from the tall grass.

The gazelles freeze in fear. They face the cheetah with their long horns pointed up toward the sky. This is a silent alarm for the herd that danger is near. The gazelles are ready to run away if the cheetah starts a chase.

CHEETAH STATS

AVERAGE HEIGHT: 2.5 feet (0.8 m) tall

AVERAGE WEIGHT: 75 to 140 pounds (34 to 64 kg)

TOP SPEED: 60 to 70 miles (97 to 113 km) per hour

THOMSON'S GAZELLE STATS

AVERAGE HEIGHT: 1.8 to 2.7 feet (0.5 to 0.8 m) tall

AVERAGE WEIGHT: 33 to 77 pounds (15 to 35 kg)

TOP SPEED: 50 miles (80 km) per hour

In a flash, the cheetah explodes into a sprint. Hooves thunder as the herd takes off. The small gazelle is struggling to keep up. Will the cheetah make this gazelle her meal?

Gazelles must run fast to avoid predators such as cheetahs.

A cheetah leaps into action.

CHAPTER 2
CHEETAH VS. GAZELLE

CHEETAHS AND THOMSON'S GAZELLES SHARE THE SAME HABITAT. They both live on the hot, dry plains of East Africa. These grassy areas with few trees are called savannas.

Cheetahs and gazelles are fast animals. Will both survive a race across the savanna? Let's compare their strengths and weaknesses to find out!

Cheetahs spend a lot of time resting.

DIET AND HUNTING HABITS

Cheetahs are carnivores. Their meals include gazelles, birds, and rabbits. Most big cats such as leopards hunt at night. But cheetahs often hunt in the morning. They eat quickly to stop other predators from stealing their food.

Thomson's gazelles are herbivores. They eat grasses, seeds, and shrubs. They sometimes feed in areas where larger animals such as wildebeests have trampled the tall grasses. This makes it easier for gazelles to eat.

A gazelle eats grass.

CHEETAH OR LEOPARD?

Both big cats have spots, but only cheetahs have two black markings on their faces called tear lines. These lines may help block bright sunlight.

SIZE

Cheetahs are about 2.5 feet (0.8 m) tall. They are smaller than lions, which are up to 4 feet (1.2 m) tall. Cheetahs' bodies are 3.7 feet to 4.7 feet (1.1 to 1.4 m) long, and their tails can be up to 2.8 feet (0.9 m) long. They use their big tails to help them balance and steer when they move.

Cheetahs are long and thin to help them run fast.

A male (*left*) and a female Thomson's gazelle

Thomson's gazelles and cheetahs are about the same height. But a male gazelle's long horns make it look taller than a cheetah. The horns can grow up to 17 inches (43 cm) long. Some females have short horns, and others have none.

GAZELLES ARE ANTELOPES

Thomson's gazelles are one of seventy-eight kinds of African antelopes. An antelope is a mammal with hooves and horns that eats plants.

STRENGTH

Cheetahs have long, strong legs that help them run fast and lunge at prey. They also have powerful jaws to clamp down on an animal's neck. They suffocate prey such as gazelles by making it impossible for them to breathe.

Young male Thomson's gazelles lock and crash their big horns together during battles. They often fight for control over an area of land or for a mate. The goal is to fight until one gazelle runs away.

A cheetah carries a dead gazelle in her jaws.

SPEED

Cheetahs are the fastest land animal on Earth. Sharp claws and ridges on their paws give them extra grip on the ground to boost their speed. Cheetahs can go from 0 to 60 miles (0 to 97 km) per hour in under three seconds! But they can only sprint at their fastest pace for about twenty seconds.

Thomson's gazelles can sprint for a short time at up to 50 miles (80 km) per hour. But they can keep running for a long time at 30 to 40 miles (48 to 64 km) per hour. Gazelles usually outrun predators that try to chase them over a long distance.

HUGE HERDS

Thomson's gazelles often live in large groups of hundreds or even over one thousand gazelles! Adult males and females usually live separately but can live in mixed herds.

A gazelle leaps in tall grass.

Cheetahs are built to sprint!

AGILITY

Cheetahs can take in a lot of air quickly with their big nostrils. This allows them to breathe more easily when they run. Cheetahs also have flexible spines that bend when they move. This helps cheetahs take long steps when sprinting. They can go 23 feet (7 m) in one stride!

MALE GAZELLES MARCH

A male Thomson's gazelle picks a mate by stretching his head toward her. Then he marches after her with straight legs.

Thomson's gazelles sometimes stot, or jump with stiff, straight legs. Experts think they may do this to tell a predator it has been seen. It may also be a way to show predators that the gazelle has the strength to outrun them. If a cheetah pursues them, gazelles run in a zigzag pattern by making several sharp turns to try to dodge an attack and escape.

A Thomson's gazelle stots.

A cheetah sneaks through dry grass.

ATTACK AND DEFENSE STYLES

Cheetahs must plan their attacks carefully. They need to make sure they won't run out of energy before catching their meal. Cheetahs try to be within 300 feet (91 m) of their prey before they start sprinting. That's about the length of one football field.

EACH CHEETAH IS UNIQUE

Just as no humans share fingerprints, no cheetahs share the same spots and tail rings. This helps conservation experts tell cheetahs apart.

Thomson's gazelles have strong senses of sight, smell, and hearing that alert them when predators are nearby. They also have sharp hooves they can dig into the ground to make quick turns at high speeds to get away. Their fur color also makes it harder to see them on the plains, which helps them hide.

A family of Thomson's gazelles blends in on the plains.

CHEETAH CHIRPS

Other big cats such as lions roar loudly to talk to one another. But cheetahs chat through chirps that sound similar to birds.

KEY WEAPONS

Cheetahs have large eyes that give them a wide view to search for prey. Their spots help them blend in with savanna grasses. This camouflage helps them secretly stalk animals before launching an attack. Then cheetahs use the strong grip of their jaws to bite or choke their prey.

By the time they are three years old, male Thomson's gazelles have grown long, curved horns. These spiked horns are covered in bumpy ridges. Male gazelles can shove a cheetah away with these sharp weapons, giving the gazelle a chance to escape. Their horns are so dangerous that male gazelles can even kill a cheetah with a deep jab.

A cheetah lies down and rests.

WEAKNESSES

Cheetahs get so tired from sprinting that they often collapse before catching their prey. Then they must recover before they can hunt again. Cheetahs also use energy to flee from predators. They run from predators such as lions because they don't have the strength to fight them.

HIDDEN CUBS

Cheetah mothers make dens in bushes or among rocks. They hide newborn cubs in the den for about six weeks to protect them.

Female Thomson's gazelles must hide their babies, or fawns, from predators. Fawns can stay still for hours. But most female gazelles do not have long horns to use as weapons. Mother gazelles usually chase away predators such as eagles rather than fight.

RISKY RIVER CROSSING

When Thomson's gazelles migrate, they must watch out for crocodiles. Crocodiles hunt gazelles when they cross rivers.

A mother gazelle (*right*) with her fawn

CHAPTER 3
WHICH ANIMAL WILL WIN?

THE CHEETAH IS SPRINTING AT NEARLY 70 MILES (113 KM) PER HOUR. But she is using a lot of energy at this speed. She can only keep up this pace for a few more seconds. She is quickly gaining on the gazelle. But gazelles are also fast on their feet. When the cheetah zigs, this gazelle zags.

The cheetah swipes at the gazelle's leg with her sharp claw. But the gazelle makes a sharp turn at high speed, leaping just out of reach.

The cheetah is running out of chances to catch her prey. She leaps up for one last attempt. She tries to sink her claws into the gazelle's back, but the gazelle shakes the cheetah off onto the ground. Then it uses its two long horns to shove the cheetah away. The cheetah gives up the chase and collapses to rest. The gazelle goes back to the herd to live another day.

RULER OF THE HABITAT

Cheetahs and gazelles are both built for speed. Cheetahs can explode in a sprint and then spring toward their prey. But gazelles are also fast runners, making quick turns at high speeds to get away. Gazelles can keep running for longer than most of their predators can. This gives gazelles a good chance of escaping from cheetahs.

Gazelles are safer when they stick together.

Cheetahs must hunt and eat other animals to live.

Although both animals live about twelve years in the wild, they each face the risk of humans hunting them. Some people hunt cheetahs for their fur. Other people catch cheetahs to sell them as pets, which is against the law. Hunters often like Thomson's gazelles for their large horns. Humans also move into places where cheetahs and gazelles live, leaving less habitat for them. But conservation groups are working to protect both animals.

The Thomson's gazelle won the battle. The cheetah tried to knock down the gazelle, but it fought back hard. Today, the gazelle rules the habitat.

PREDATOR VS. PREY: HEAD-TO-HEAD

CHEETAH

- Sharp claws and ridged paws for running fast
- Strong jaws to choke prey

THOMSON'S GAZELLE

- Runs long distances to tire out predators
- Locks and clashes horns during fights between males

GLOSSARY

carnivore: an animal that eats other animals

conservation: planned management of a natural resource to prevent exploitation, pollution, destruction, or neglect

habitat: the place where a plant or animal naturally lives or grows

herbivore: an animal that eats plants

mammal: a warm-blooded animal that nourishes its young with milk and has skin usually covered with hair

mate: one in a pair of animals that comes together to produce young

migrate: to move from one place to another to find food and water

predator: an animal that hunts other animals to eat

prey: an animal hunted by another animal for food

sense: a way that an animal sees, hears, feels, tastes, or smells its surroundings

LEARN MORE

Bulion, Leslie. *Serengeti: Plains of Grass*. Atlanta: Peachtree, 2021.

National Geographic Kids: Cheetah
https://kids.nationalgeographic.com/animals/mammals/facts/cheetah

National Geographic Kids: Save Our Savannahs!
https://www.natgeokids.com/uk/home-is-good/savannah-habitat/

Riggs, Kate. *Cheetahs*. Mankato, MN: Creative Education, 2025.

Smithsonian's National Zoo & Conservation Biology Institute: Cheetah
https://nationalzoo.si.edu/animals/cheetah

Winter, Steve. *The Ultimate Book of Big Cats: Your Guide to the Secret Lives of These Fierce, Fabulous Felines*. Washington, DC: National Geographic Kids, 2022.

INDEX

PHOTO ACKNOWLEDGMENTS

Image credits: Li Jia/Getty Images, pp. 4–5; wellsie82/Getty Images, p. 6; Mark Chivers/Getty Images, p. 7 (top); Marie Lemerle/Alamy, p. 7 (bottom); Anton_Petrus/Getty Images, p. 8; GP232/Getty Images, p. 9; dagut/Getty Images, pp. 10–11; Design Pics Inc/Alamy, p. 12; Ibrahim Suha Derbent/Getty Images, pp. 13, 28; David DesRochers/Alamy, p. 14; Stu Porter/Alamy, p. 15; Russell Burden/Getty Images, p. 16; slowmotiongli/Getty Images, p. 17; Laura Romin & Larry Dalton/Alamy, p. 18; Carlos A Carreno/c3.photos via Getty Images, p. 19; Jane Rix/Alamy, p. 20; Alberto Carrera/Getty Images, p. 21; Moelyn Photos/Getty Images, p. 22; Imagebroker/Alamy, p. 23; © Winfried Wisniewski/Minden Pictures, pp. 24–25; Ignacio Palacios/Getty Images, p. 26; WLDavies/Getty Images, p. 27; robertharding/Alamy, p. 29. Design elements: iunewind/Shutterstock; Milano M/Shutterstock; Cassel/Shutterstock; Textures and backgrounds/Shutterstock; Print Net/Shutterstock; Ukrainian studio/Shutterstock.

Cover images: Joe Petersburger/Getty Images; Bernd Wesner/500px/Getty Images.